Unit 6
Adventures

Contents

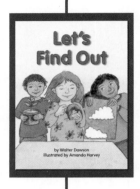

Week 1

Let's Find Out I
/ů/: vowel digraph *oo*; /ü/: vowel
digraphs *oo, ew, ue, ou*; *u_e*

Realistic Fiction

Show What You Know

Olivia................................... 9
/ů/: vowel digraph *oo*; /ü/: vowel
digraphs *oo, ew, ue, ou*; *u_e*
possessives

Informational Text

Week 2

All for Paul II
/ô/: vowel digraphs *au, aw, augh, al; a*

Realistic Fiction

Show What You Know

Peter and Willie I7
/ô/: vowel digraphs *au, aw, augh, al; a*
singular and plural possessive pronouns

Informational Text

Week 3

Born to Fly 19
words with prefixes *un-*, *re-*
Biography (Literary Nonfiction)

Show What You Know

Cool Jobs 27
words with prefixes *un-*, *re-*
r-controlled /ârl: air, are, ear
Informational Text

The Painting Problem

by Meish Goldish
illustrated by Peggy Tagel

Week 4

The Painting Problem 29
open and closed syllables

Realistic Fiction

Show What You Know

Dot and Jabber 35
open and closed syllables
contractions

Informational Text

Week 5

The Birthday Party.......... 37
final stable syllables

Fiction

Show What You Know

Super Oscar 43
final stable syllables
compound words

Informational Text

Let's Find Out

by Walter Dawson
illustrated by Amanda Harvey

Mrs. Booth's room is planning
a "Let's Find Out" day.
We are sitting in a small group.
We will tell what we plan to do.

Joe will bring flowers that
he grew.
Joy will show her drawings
of clouds and blue sky.

I'll bring my new pet mouse, Sue.
She is good at learning to
crawl in a maze.
I trained her to find food.

4

The next day, I take Sue to
school in a huge box.
But when I open the box, she
is gone!

We check and recheck
the classroom.
"Come on, Sue," I yell.
"Don't spoil my plan."
6   The kids help me look.

Our "Let's Find Out" day is renamed
"Let's Find Sue" day!
I don't think we will ever find Sue.
Now I see June point.

June finds my mouse!
The day turns out fine.
But now Mrs. Booth will
rethink the new rule.
No more pets in school!

Olivia

Things True About Olivia

1. She brushes her teeth with a red toothbrush.
2. She tries on more than a few dresses and shirts!
3. She makes a large painting in her room.
4. She reads three good books with her mom.
5. She is good at wearing people out!

9

Things NOT True About Olivia

1. She sings sweet tunes in a soft voice.
2. She plays with her brother a lot.
3. She takes a nap each day at noon.
4. She gets into bed at night without a fuss.
5. She likes to sit still! Do you?

My New Words

look	stood	food	June	group
soon	soup	flute	knew	girl's
chew	new	blue	through	dad's

All for Paul

by Meish Goldish
illustrated by Ronnie Rooney

Dawn always played ball with Paul on the lawn. One day, Paul threw the ball high and Dawn caught it.

Then Dawn threw the small
ball too hard. It wasn't her
fault. It caused the ball to go
past Paul. Dawn saw it go in
the street.   13

Paul ran to scoop up the ball.
Dawn called, "No, Paul!
Don't get the ball! Stay on
the lawn!"

Dawn ran to stop Paul. She grabbed Paul's legs and stuck to him like glue. Dawn made Paul fall. Mother and Father ran outside.

"Nice job, Dawn!" Mother said. "You saved Paul!"

"I love Paul," said Dawn. "I always want him to be safe."

Peter and Willie

Peter

Peter saw a boy whistle for his dog.

Peter tries to whistle too, but he can't do it.

He can whirl and twirl without falling.

Peter keeps trying until he does it!

Now he whistles all the time!

Willie

Willie is a small dog with dark brown fur.

He has a long body, short legs, and little paws.

He is Peter's best pal.

When Peter whistles, Willie runs to him.

My New Words

wall	salt	launch	walk	fault
straw	dawn	sauce	caught	taught
gnaw	also	hers	their	theirs

Born to Fly

by Maryann Dobeck
illustrated by Steven Marchesi

Orville and Wilbur Wright

Some say Orville and Wilbur
Wright were born to fly.
Their 1903 flight was
the first of its kind.

As children the boys got along well.
One night their dad came home
early with a present for them.
He tossed it up high.

Did it just fall and drop?
No, instead it sped right by!
Why? It had rubber bands to
wind up.

As the bands unwound,
the toy flew.
That flying toy might have
started a big dream.

As grown-ups the men had
a real goal. They wanted to
make the first plane and fly it.
The men worked hard.

Would the plane fly and return
to land? Or would it crash?
The first test flights didn't go
well. But the men weren't
unhappy. They still had hope.

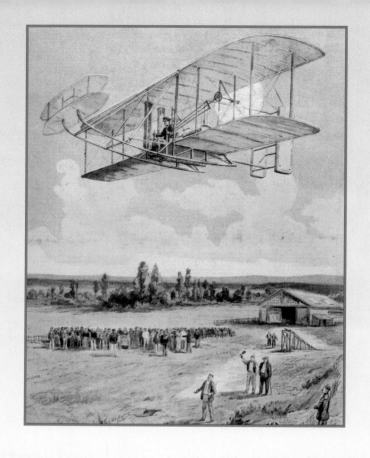

They found a way to fix the
problems. In the winter of
1903, they got their plane to fly.
What a sight it was to see
a plane flying like a bird!

26

Cool Jobs

A zoo dentist has a cool job! These dentists fix and clean a tiger's or a lion's teeth. Animals with unhealthy teeth will be quite unhappy! But zoo dentists take good care of them. Is the job unsafe? No—the animals get medicine that lets them sleep as the dentist works.

27

A beekeeper's job is cool, too! Beekeepers make hives out of wood. These hives replace the hives that the bees make. When beekeepers open the hives to take out honey, their outfit keeps them safe. Helping bees make honey is a sweet job!

My New Words

reread	reuse	unlock	unkind	wear
fair	hair	square	dare	share
bear	chair	pear	stairs	repair

The Painting Problem

by Meish Goldish
illustrated by Peggy Tagel

Mark goes to Steph's yard
to play. They like the fresh
air and have fun building a
wooden home.

30

Mark and Steph finish.
Steph says, "Now we need to
paint the outside."
"Let's begin!" Mark says.

Steph says, "Let's paint the outside green."
Mark begins to laugh.
"We can't," he says. "We only have blue and yellow paint."

"That's no problem," says
Steph. "Watch this."
Mark stares while Steph mixes
the blue and yellow paint.
"It's green!" Mark shouts.

"That's correct," says Steph.
"Mixing blue and yellow
makes green."
"I never knew that!" says Mark.
"We make a good pair!"

Dot and Jabber

The bugs vanish, and Dot decides to look for them.

A rabbit explains to Dot why bugs and toads hide.

Now Dot sees lots of bugs and grasshoppers.

Dot looks at them crawl away as fast as they can.

Dot finds out that bugs and animals hide in plain sight!

Jabber thinks the bugs might be invisible.

He sees a bird sitting on a branch.

Jabber believes the bugs are watching him and Dot.

He finds a toad between some rocks.

Jabber hides in plain sight and asks Dot to find him!

My New Words

napkin	picnic	cabin	contest	dentist
paper	below	report	before	lady
I've	they're	let's	don't	we're

The Birthday Party

Happy Birthday!

by **Meish Goldish**
illustrated by **Jannie Ho**

Betty was very happy.
Today was her birthday. She
had been planning a little
party all week. She had many
games for her friends to play.

Many children came to the party. "Let's play Pin the Tail on the Kitten," Betty said. "I just need to get the blindfold."

Betty looked for the
blindfold. She wasn't able to
find it. "I don't know where
it's gone," she said.

The children began
searching, too. They looked
behind the couch. They
looked under the rug. The
blindfold was missing.

Then the cat came in.
"Look!" shouted Betty. "Kitty
has it! She wants to play Pin
the Tail on the Kitten, too!"

Super Oscar

Oscar's Daydreams

1. In the morning, Oscar daydreamed at breakfast.
2. He dreamed about flying in a spaceship.
3. He dreamed about riding on a huge dinosaur.
4. In the middle of the day, he daydreamed some more.
5. On the weekend, he looked at the clouds and daydreamed.

Oscar's Picnic

1. Oscar raced to the supermarket and got lots of food.
2. He ran to the park and set the picnic tables.
3. He whipped the cream for strawberry shortcake.
4. Oscar made a super picnic!

My New Words

giggle	simple	puddle	bubble
puzzle	turtle	circle	raindrop
popcorn	snapshot	bedroom	sidewalk

Unit 6: Adventures

to use with *Olivia*   **WORD COUNT: 153**

DECODABLE WORDS
Target Phonics Elements
/ü/ *ew*
   grew, new
/ü/ *oo*
   Booth, Booth's, classroom, food, room
/ů/ *oo*
   good, look
/ü/ *ou*
   group
/ü/ *u_e*
   June, rule
/u/ *ue*
   blue, Sue

Words Using Previously Taught Skills
a, and, at, box, bring, but, check, clouds, day, don't, ever, find(s), fine, flowers, he, help, her, huge, I, I'll, in, is, Joe, Joy, kids, let's, maze, me, Mrs., more, mouse, my, next, no, now, on, open, our, out, pet(s), plan, planning, point, recheck, renamed, rethink, see, she, show, sitting, sky, spoil, take, tell, that, the, think, trained, turns, we, when, will, yell

HIGH-FREQUENCY WORDS
Review: are, come, do, learning, of, school, to, what

STORY WORDS
crawl, drawings, gone, small

SHOW WHAT YOU KNOW: Olivia

DECODABLE WORDS
Target Phonics Elements
/ů/ *oo*; /u/ *oo, ew, u_e, ue, ou*
possessives
   blue, books, chew, dad's, few, flute, food, girl's, good, group, June, knew, look, new, noon, room, soon, soup, stood, through, toothbrush, true, tunes, you

45

Week 2: All for Paul *page 11*

to use with *Whistle for Willie*   **WORD COUNT: 105**

DECODABLE WORDS

Target Phonics Elements

/ô/ a, al
all, always, ball, called, fall, small

/ô/ au, augh
caught, caused, fault, Paul, Paul's

/ô/ aw
Dawn, lawn, saw

Words Using Previously Taught Skills
and, be, day, don't, for, get, glue, go, grabbed, hard, her, high, him, his, I, in, it, job, legs, like, made, nice, no, on, outside, past, played, ran, safe, saved, scoop, she, stay, stop, street, stuck, the, then, threw, too, up, with, you

HIGH-FREQUENCY WORDS

Review: Father, love, Mother, one, said, to, want, wasn't

SHOW WHAT YOU KNOW: Peter and Willie

DECODABLE WORDS

Target Phonics Elements

/ô/ a, al, au, aw, augh

singular and plural possessive pronouns
(my/mine, you/yours, her/hers)
all, also, caught, dawn, falling, fault, gnaw, hers, his, launch, paws, salt, sauce, saw, small, straw, taught, their, theirs, walk, wall

Week 3: Born to Fly *page 19*

to use with *Cool Jobs*   **WORD COUNT: 162**

DECODABLE WORDS

Target Phonics Element

2-syllable words; words with prefixes *un-*, *re-*
along, children, didn't, flying, grown-ups, instead, Orville, present, problems, return, rubber, started, unhappy, unwound, Wilbur, winter

46

Words Using Previously Taught Skills

a, and, as, bands, big, bird, born, boys, but, by, came, crash, dad, did, dream, drop, fall, first, fix, flew, flight(s), fly, for, found, go, goal, got, had, hard, he, high, home, hope, in, it, its, just, kind, land, like, make, men, might, night, no, or, plane, real, right, say, see, sight, sped, still, test, that, the, them, tossed, toy, up, way, well, why, wind, with, Wright

HIGH-FREQUENCY WORDS

Review: early, have, of, one, some, their, they, to, want(ed), was, were, weren't, what, worked, would

SHOW WHAT YOU KNOW: Cool Jobs

DECODABLE WORDS

Target Phonics Elements

2-syllable words; words with prefixes *un-*, *re-*

r-controlled /âr/ *air, are, ear*

bear, care, chair, dare, dentist(s), fair, hair, helping, honey, lion's, open, outfit, pear, repair, replace, reread, reuse, share, square, stairs, tiger's, unhappy, unhealthy, unkind, unlock, unsafe, wear

Week 4: The Painting Problem   *page 29*

to use with *Dot and Jabber and the Big Bug Mystery*   **WORD COUNT: 100**

DECODABLE WORDS

Target Phonics Element

2-syllable words; open and closed syllables

begin(s), correct, finish, mixes, mixing, never, only, outside, painting, problem, wooden, yellow

Words Using Previously Taught Skills

a, air, and, blue, can't, fresh, fun, goes, good, green, he, home, I, it's, knew, let's, like, make(s), Mark, need, no, now, paint, pair, play, shouts, stares, Steph, Steph's, that, that's, the, this, we, while, yard

HIGH-FREQUENCY WORDS

Review: build(ing), have, laugh, says, they, to

SHOW WHAT YOU KNOW: Dot and Jabber

DECODABLE WORDS

Target Phonics Elements

2-syllable words; open and closed syllables

contractions

away, before, believes, below, between, cabin, contest, decides, dentist, don't, explains, I've, Jabber, lady, let's, napkin, paper, picnic, rabbit, report, sitting, they're, vanish, watching, we're

Week 5: The Birthday Party   *page 37*

to use with *Super Oscar*   **WORD COUNT: 109**

DECODABLE WORDS

Target Phonics Element

2-syllable words; final stable syllables

able, before, began, behind, Betty, birthday, blindfold, children, happy, kitten, Kitty, little, missing, party, planning, shouted, today, under

Words Using Previously Taught Skills

a, all, came, cat, couch, don't, find, for, games, get, had, has, her, I, in, it, it's, just, know, let's, look, looked, need, on, pin, play, rug, she, tail, the, then, too, week

HIGH-FREQUENCY WORDS

Review: been, friends, gone, many, said, searching, they, to, very, wants, was, wasn't, where

SHOW WHAT YOU KNOW: Super Oscar

DECODABLE WORDS

Target Phonics Elements

2-syllable words; final stable syllables

compound words

about, bedroom, breakfast, bubble, circle, daydreamed, daydreams, flying, giggle, middle, morning, Oscar('s), picnic, popcorn, puddle, puzzle, raindrop, riding, shortcake, sidewalk, simple, snapshot, spaceship, strawberry, super, supermarket, tables, turtle, weekend

HIGH-FREQUENCY WORDS TAUGHT TO DATE

Grade K	Grade I				
a	about	climbed	into	people	under
and	across	come	it	place	up
are	after	could	jump	poor	upon
can	again	does	knew	pretty	use
do	against	done	know	pull	very
for	air	down	laugh	put	walked
go	all	early	learn	ride	want
has	along	eat	live	run	warm
have	also	eight	love	saw	water
he	always	enough	make	says	way
here	another	every	many	school	were
I	any	eyes	minutes	searching	who
is	around	fall	more	should	why
like	away	father	mother	shout	work
little	ball	find	move	show	would
look	be	four	never	so	write
me	because	friends	new	some	yellow
my	been	from	no	soon	your
play	before	full	not	sound	
said	begin	funny	nothing	straight	
see	below	girl	now	sure	
she	better	give	of	their	
the	blue	gone	old	then	
this	boy	goes	once	there	
to	brought	good	one	they	
was	build	great	only	thought	
we	buy	grew	open	three	
what	by	head	or	through	
where	call	help	orange	today	
with	carry	her	other	together	
you	certain	house	our	too	
	change	how	out	two	
		instead	over	until	

49

DECODING SKILLS TAUGHT TO DATE

CVC letter patterns; short *a*; consonants *b, c, ck, f, g, h, k, l, m, n, p, r, s, t, v;* inflectional ending *-s* (plurals, verbs); short *i*; consonants *d, j, qu, w, x, y, z;* double final consonants; *l* blends; possessives with *'s;* end blends; short *o;* inflectional ending *-ed;* short *e;* contractions with *n't; s* blends; *r* blends; inflectional ending *-ing;* short *u;* contractions with *'s;* digraphs *sh, th, ng;* compound words; long *a (a_e),* inflectional ending *-ed* (drop final *e*); long *i (i_e);* soft *c, g, -dge;* digraphs *ch, -tch, wh-, ph;* inflectional ending *-es* (no change to base word); long *e (e_e),* long *o (o_e),* long *u (u_e);* silent letters *gn, kn, wr;* 3-letter blends *scr-, spl-, spr-, str-;* inflectional endings *-ed, -ing* (double final consonant); long *a (ai, ay);* inflectional endings *-er, -est;* long *e (e, ea, ee, ie); e* at the end of long *e* words; long *o (o, oa, oe, ow);* 2-syllable words; long *i (i, ie, igh, y);* 2-syllable inflectional endings (changing *y* to *ie*); long *e (ey, y);* inflectional ending *-ed* (verbs; change *y* to *i*); *r*-controlled vowel /ûr/*er, ir, ur;* inflectional endings *-er, -est* (drop final *e*); *r*-controlled vowel /är/*ar;* abbreviations Mr., Mrs., Dr.; *r*-controlled vowel /ôr/*or, oar, ore; ea* as short *e;* diphthong /ou/*ou, ow;* final *e* (mouse, house); diphthong /oi/*oi, oy;* prefixes *re-, un-;* /ù̇/: vowel digraph *oo;* /ü/: vowel digraphs *oo, ew, ue, ou; u_e;* possessives; /ô/: vowel digraph, *au, aw, augh, al; a;* singular and plural possessive pronouns; 2-syllable words; *r*-controlled vowel /âr/*air, are, ear;* contractions; open syllables; closed syllables; final stable syllables; vowel digraph syllables; *r*-controlled vowel syllables; vowel diphthong syllables

Photography

Cover, I: Nicki Pardo/Getty Images. 20: Bettmann/Corbis. 23: Library of Congress, Prints & Photographs Division, [LC-DIG-ppprs-00580]. 24: Tim Wimbourne/Reuters.